MW00888109

This Notebook Belongs To:

___

Made in United States
Troutdale, OR
07/31/2023

11714492R00069